TEXAS
BIGGER AND
BRIGHTER

50 ICONIC LONE STAR PEOPLE, PLACES, AND THINGS

Donna Ingham
Photographs by Paul Porter

LONE
STAR
BOOKS

Guilford, Connecticut
Helena, Montana

An imprint of Globe Pequot
An imprint and registered trademark of Rowman & Littlefield

Distributed by NATIONAL BOOK NETWORK

All photos by Paul Porter except: Donna Ingham, pages x (top left), 2–3, 23–24, 48–49, and 85 (top two); Texas Department of Transportation, page 79; Texas Historical Commission, page 80

British Library Cataloguing in Publication Information available

A previous edition was catalogued by the Library of Congress as follows:

Library of Congress Cataloging-in-Publication Data

Ingham, Donna.
Texas icons : 50 classic views of the lone star state / Donna Ingham ; with photographs by Paul Porter.
p. cm.
ISBN 978-0-7627-7336-7
1. Texas—Miscellanea. 2. Texas—Pictorial works. I. Title.
F387.I56 2012
976.40022'2—dc23

2011043854

ISBN 978-1-4930-2410-0 (hardcover)
ISBN 978-1-4930-2411-7 (e-book)

Printed in Malaysia

For my favorite traveling companions:
Jerry, Christopher, and Stephanie

CONTENTS

INTRODUCTION

If in some distant millennia archaeologists were to excavate Texas, what would they find in the way of meaningful artifacts, structures, and other relics to suggest the uniqueness of Texan life and culture? Icons, to be sure—that is, actual images of significant people preserved in bronze and marble and cement: political leaders, artists, heroes of one sort or another. Remnants of buildings and monuments with domes and towers and obelisks. Fossils of animals and seeds of fruits and flowers. Well, you get the idea.

Meanwhile, in the here and now, the evidence is in full view that Texas is a special place. It is celebrated for its basics: barbecue and Tex-Mex, boots and jeans and cowboy hats, pickup trucks, the Alamo, oil wells, longhorns, and bluebonnets. It is recognized for its distinctive shape and its diversity of landscape. From Palo Duro Canyon to the Big Bend and from the Rio Grande to Caddo Lake, there are mountains and plains, desert and swamp. It has a history that dates back to early Spanish missions and carries forward to missions into space coordinated from the Johnson Space Center. It clings to its Lone Star, a reminder that Texas was once its own republic, and Texans can (and will) boast about a fairly long list of biggest, tallest, longest, most, first, and only.

They'll tell you, for example, that Texas has more bird species than any other state or province in North America, that Brenham's Blue Bell homemade vanilla is the best-selling single flavor of ice cream in the United States, that Dr Pepper is the No. 1 non-cola soft drink in the country, that Huntsville's statue of Sam Houston is the world's largest statue of any American hero and the San Jacinto Monument is the world's tallest war memorial, that the Kerrville Folk Festival is the largest and longest-running festival of its kind in the United States, and that the King Ranch is the largest cattle ranch in the country. Taken together, San Antonio's missions are the largest concentration of Catholic missions in North America; the Texas State Capitol is the largest in the nation, and its dome is higher than the one on the national capitol; Texas is the largest producer of oil and gas in the United States and the nation's leader in pickup sales; and its wind farms are the largest in the world.

To further call attention to itself and its cultural icons, Texas is prone to making those icons "official." So, for example, there is an official state flower, the bluebonnet, and there are official state mammals, the longhorn (large) and the armadillo (small). The mockingbird is the state bird, and the Ruby Red grapefruit is the state fruit. Texas even has a state dinosaur, the *Pleurocoelus*.

Bragging rights aside, however, Texas has any number of hidden treasures and downright quirky attractions. Its state parks and natural areas feature everything from a bison herd to a giant rock called a batholith to a gateway to a presidential ranch.

Some of its 254 county courthouses are architectural marvels. Other man-made landmarks, such as the Fort Worth Stockyards, pay tribute to a past era or, like Neiman Marcus, recognize the entrepreneurial spirit of more modern citified folks.

Coyotes still wail along the trail, and rattlesnakes den up in the desert. Quarter horses are prized on ranches and racetracks alike. It's still possible to eat chuck off a wagon and see real cowboys working real cattle. Then there's that Cadillac Ranch up in the Panhandle.

For fun, why not take in the Texas State Fair, ride the Texas State Railroad, smell the Tyler roses, stroll along San Antonio's River Walk, or take a dip in one of Texas's many natural swimming holes? Museums and larger-than-life statues honor native sons and daughters such as Lyndon B. Johnson, Barbara Jordan, Buddy Holly, and J. Frank Dobie.

All of these and more are cataloged in the pages of this book, so we hope you enjoy the tour. These are just for starters, of course; any Texan in any town along the way will be ready to add personal favorites to the list—just trying to be helpful and live up to the official state motto: friendship.

THE ALAMO

In the end, it was a bunch of women who rallied to "Remember the Alamo" and saved it from possible destruction. That was at the beginning of the twentieth century, but the mission-turned-fortress had been threatened at least twice before, in the nineteenth century.

First it was Sam Houston, the Texas general who was not at the famous battle between Texan and Mexican forces on March 6, 1836, who suggested it would be better to "blow up the Alamo and abandon the place." Retreat was not an option, however, in the minds of those who stayed to become martyrs to the cause of Texas independence.

As everyone knows, they lost the battle, and then it was the victorious Mexican general Antonio López de Santa Anna who ordered the Alamo destroyed. According to legend, ghostly sentries appeared to hold the demolition details at bay.

Not long after its defining moment in history, however, what is now the most revered historic site in Texas became a victim of neglect and by the end of the nineteenth century had fallen into serious disrepair.

Then came Clara Driscoll, daughter of a multimillionaire, granddaughter of two veterans of the Texas Revolution, and committed to historic preservation. She teamed up with the Daughters of the Republic of Texas between 1903 and 1905 to acquire and preserve the Alamo. Driscoll paid most of the purchase price herself and quickly became known as the "Savior of the Alamo."

The familiar facade pictured on postcards today is actually built some distance from where the original San Antonio de Valero Mission was established in 1718 as a way station between the Rio Grande and the Spanish missions in east Texas. The chapel left standing in what is now downtown San Antonio was constructed in 1750.

Historians still can't agree on the source of the name *Alamo*. Some say it came from a nearby grove of cotton woods (*álamo* in Spanish), others that it referred to a company of soldiers housed at the mission in 1803 from Álamo de Parras in Mexico.

What is certain is that the Alamo remains a central symbol of Texas and attracts 2.5 million visitors a year.

The Alamo | 300 Alamo Plaza | San Antonio, TX 78205 | (210) 225-1391 | thealamo.org

ARMADILLO

In Texas, not only chickens cross the road. So do armadillos, at their peril. For although armadillos have few natural enemies, humans are among them—especially humans in automobiles. Highway traffic poses a deadly hazard, especially because armadillos, when startled, spring several feet into the air, about grille-high to an oncoming car.

Whether roadkill or live, the ungainly critters look as if they might have been designed by a government committee. About the size and weight of a large cat, they appear to be downright prehistoric—which they are—with their distinctive armor-like shell. They are the only remaining mammals with a shell, which is actually two shields, one over the shoulders and one over the rump, with nine bands in the middle. Thus the name of the Texas species: the nine-banded armadillo.

Partial to insects of all sorts—even fire ants—and the occasional worm or small reptile, armadillos have supersensitive noses that can sniff out a tasty meal six inches underground. They have sharp claws and are prolific burrowers, making them unwelcome guests in people's lawns.

Armadillos thrive everywhere in Texas except in the state's arid regions. They like water, although they can't swim worth a hoot. No problem, though. If a creek is narrow enough, an armadillo simply holds its breath and walks along the bottom under water. To cross a wider river, an armadillo gulps in enough air to inflate its stomach and intestines like a balloon and floats across.

Armadillos have been giving up their shells for the Texas souvenir trade since the late nineteenth century, when the armadillo-shell basket was invented. The shells have also been fashioned into lamp shades, purses, and other curios.

For the sports minded, there are armadillo races, dating back to the early 1950s, but handling armadillos can be a little risky. They are the only mammals, other than humans, known to carry Hansen's disease, or leprosy. For this reason, it is illegal to sell a live armadillo in Texas.

Nevertheless, Texans have adopted the curious little beast as a mascot of sorts, and in 1995, the Seventy-fourth Legislature designated the armadillo as the state's official small mammal.

Texas Wild! Petting Corral | Fort Worth Zoo
1989 Colonial Pkwy. | Fort Worth, TX 76110 | (817) 759-7555 | fortworthzoo.org

BARBECUE

By and large, barbecue specialists in Texas seem to gravitate to small towns and open small establishments. The purists build aboveground "pits" out of metal or bricks and stoke them with mesquite, oak, hickory, or pecan. They get the fires going at about three in the morning and may smoke a brisket for ten to fifteen hours or more until it is fall-apart tender—moist on the inside and crusty on the outside.

For although it is possible to order pork ribs or chops or sausage or chicken or even mutton or goat at a Texas barbecue joint, beef is the defining meat, and brisket is the cut of choice.

Carnivorous connoisseurs follow smoke and smell. They look for pickup trucks parked out front, are willing to stand in long lines, and order their meat by the pound. They fancy places with a smoky patina on the wall and settle for no-frills service: sheets of white butcher paper for plates and a roll of paper towels for cleanup.

The standard sides are cheap white sandwich bread, pinto beans, potato salad, and coleslaw. Barbecue sauce is optional and generally served on the side. It tends to be thin, tart, and vinegary, with a tomato and chili powder base. Desserts are almost always peach or berry cobblers, or sometimes banana pudding.

Texas barbecue is a high-flavor delight and a low-tech operation. A good pit master doesn't need a thermometer to know when the meat is done. He or she knows how it is supposed to look and smell and sizzle and is willing to give the smoking the attention it deserves. There are no shortcuts and nothing fast about this food.

So it's always a good idea to plan ahead and arrive early, as most places stay open only until the meat runs out.

Sonny Bryan's Smokehouse
2202 Inwood Rd. | Dallas, TX 75235 | (214) 357-7120 | sonnybryans.com

Stubb's Barbecue | 801 Red River St. | Austin, TX 78701
(512) 480-8341 | stubbsaustin.com

and many, many more . . .

BIG BEND

To say Big Bend National Park is big is an understatement. It's about the size of Rhode Island, and its 801,000 acres encompass massive canyons, the entire Chisos Mountain range, vast expanses of the Chihuahuan Desert, a 118-mile stretch of the Rio Grande, and 150 miles of unpaved roads. Now that's big.

But the name of the park actually comes from its location in a great southward swing, or bend, of the Rio Grande, which borders it on three sides. Along the river are three particularly noteworthy canyons: Santa Elena, Mariscal, and Boquillas. The park harbors more than fifty-eight endangered and threatened plant and animal species and more than 430 species of birds.

Some of the most spectacular views in Big Bend are on the trails up the southern edge of

the Chisos Mountains. Mind-blowing scenery along and below the South Rim reveals extremes from desolate badlands to shady forests. One trail fork goes to Emory Peak, the highest point in the Chisos at 7,832 feet. A less demanding trail is the one to Santa Elena Canyon, where thousand-foot rock walls rise from the Rio Grande.

Established in 1944, Big Bend was the first national park in Texas, and from the start the National Park Service recognized the landscape as "decidedly the outstanding scenic area in Texas."

To this day the NPS proposes only basic improvements, thus allowing the park's natural zones to "remain largely unaltered by human activity." That means hardier campers can claim a space that has no amenities, no lights, possibly no neighbors, and no noise.

Big Bend country lies south of the Davis Mountains in far west Texas and appeals especially to those who really want to get away from it all. The whole region is unpopulated to the point of downright isolation, presenting a likely backdrop for a western movie. Enough inns and restaurants are open in what pockets of civilization there are, however, to provide creature comforts for those who don't want to truly rough it.

And just in case the expanse of the national park is not enough, there's always Big Bend Ranch State Park nearby. With almost three hundred thousand acres, it extends along the Rio Grande from southeast of Presidio to near Lajitas.

Big Bend National Park | PO Box 129
Big Bend National Park, TX 79834 | (432) 477-2251 | nps.gov/bibe

BIRDING

South Texas in particular is decidedly for the birds—or so the birders who flock there every year would say. Dotted along 120 miles of the Rio Grande, from South Padre Island to Roma, are nine sites composing the World Birding Center, where visitors can look for more than five hundred species of birds that inhabit or migrate through the area. Even longer is the Great Coastal Birding Trail, extending along the entire length of the Texas Gulf coast. At 2,110 miles, it is the longest in the land, and *Audubon* magazine touts it as one of the best in the nation.

Texas can boast having more bird species than any other state or province in North America. They funnel through the Rio Grande valley on their journeys south in the fall and north in the spring. And some just stay, such as the green jays that cross the border from Mexico.

Farther north, in the Hill Country, the endangered golden-cheeked warblers fledge from nests in central Texas. The warblers breed entirely within the state's boundaries. To the east the red-cockaded woodpecker, also on the endangered species list, is a resident in the Piney Woods.

One of the most watched-for birds is the whooping crane. The tallest of all North American birds, the cranes stand nearly five feet, and

their survival is quite a success story. In 1941 they faced extinction, numbering only fifteen in one flock wintering at what was then the Aransas Migratory Waterfowl Refuge.

Texans took note and took action, as did Canadians, since the whoopers nest in northern Canada—roughly 2,400 miles away. Thus began what has been called "a love affair of two nations with a great white bird."

Although still endangered, the cranes' numbers have dramatically increased, thanks to better protection of habitat and a program to raise

some of the birds in captivity. They make it back to winter in Texas each year, landing in what is now Aransas National Wildlife Refuge on a broad peninsula about twelve miles across Aransas Bay northeast of Rockport. The best time to see them is from late October or November through March.

Visitors can get a good view from an observation platform at the refuge or on a boat trip in Aransas Bay.

World Birding Center Headquarters | Bentsen–Rio Grande Valley State Park
2800 S. Bentsen Palm Dr. (FM 2062) | Mission, TX 78572
(956) 584-9156 | theworldbirdingcenter.com/bentsen.html

US Fish and Wildlife Service Aransas National Wildlife Refuge Complex
PO Box 100 | Austwell, TX 77950 | (361) 286-3559 | fws.gov/southwest/refuges/texas/aransas

BLUE BELL ICE CREAM

The president and CEO of Blue Bell Creameries claims he has to taste as many as eighty flavors of ice cream a day. It's a tough job, but somebody's got to do it. He prefers to do his tasting in the afternoon rather than the morning, he says, because he swallows every bite. His favorite is still Homemade Vanilla, Blue Bell's best seller. Introduced in 1969, the Blue Bell version is in fact the best-selling single flavor of ice cream in the United States.

At first the Brenham Creamery Company, as it was called in the beginning, made only butter. Characterizing itself as "the little creamery in Brenham," it opened its doors in 1907 and began cranking out a gallon or two of ice cream per day, one batch at a time, by 1911.

The company makes its own deliveries, starting first with a horse and wagon, then trading up to a horseless carriage in the late 1920s. By 1930 the company had taken its new name, Blue Bell Creameries, from a wildflower that grew in the area, and by 1936 it had its first refrigerated delivery truck and its first assembly line–style ice cream freezer, which produced a continuous flow of ice cream that could fill containers at a rate of eighty gallons per hour.

These days, in addition to creating new flavors for the tasters to sample, Blue Bell routinely produces more than twenty tried-and-true flavors year-round, rotating some in and out every three months, and another twenty or more flavors seasonally. Cookies 'n' Cream? Blue Bell made it first.

Fortunately, Brenham is right smack-dab in the middle of Texas dairy country, because it takes between forty thousand and fifty thousand cows to provide the milk used on a daily basis to make Blue Bell ice cream.

The company's advertising slogan is "We eat all we can and we sell the rest." That arrangement apparently works well enough for Blue Bell to be the number-one ice cream in Texas and one of the top three sellers nationwide. It's about as close to hand-cranked good as a body can get.

Blue Bell Creameries | 1101 S. Blue Bell Rd. | Brenham, TX 77833
(800) 327-8135 | bluebell.com

BOOTS AND JEANS
AND COWBOY HATS

When people get to thinking about how the West was worn, they picture boots and jeans and cowboy hats, and in Texas those items still make a fashion statement.

Working cowboys and cowgirls wear them for practical reasons. A boot's high top protects the lower legs. Its pointed toe helps guide the foot into a saddle stirrup, and the high heel keeps the foot from slipping all the way through the stirrup while the cowhand is riding the range.

Denim jeans are heavy enough to protect the legs and snug enough to prevent the pants legs from snagging on brush, corral equipment, and other hazards. And the broad-brimmed cowboy hat provides shade, blocks rain, and even fans fires.

Meanwhile, those whose stomping grounds may be a courtroom, a boardroom, or a cubicle may opt to wear well-shined boots with their three-piece suits or starched and creased jeans with blazers and ties or even tuxedo jackets. Womenfolk in Texas don their fashion jeans with high heels, fancy blouses and jackets, and expensive jewelry—especially that made from silver and turquoise. That's for highfalutin occasions. For daily wear a pair of casual jeans with boots or half-boots will do.

Hats can be felt or straw, depending on the season. Brims range from four to five inches, and crown styles can be flat, pinched, or creased. The finishing touch is the hatband—a design as simple as a felt strip matching the hat color or as distinctive as braided leather or even a gold-and-diamond chain. Regional preferences lean toward turquoise-studded bands in west Texas and silver conchos in south Texas. Some cowgirls request tassels or feathers.

The phrase "ten-gallon hat," by the way, has nothing to do with gallons at all. It comes from the Spanish word *gallon,* meaning "braid," and has come to mean an elaborately decorated or extra-big hat.

Texas Bootmakers List | texas-best.com/texas-bootmakers-list

BUFFALO

With a state park as a home, the buffalo still roam in Texas. The Texas State Bison Herd now grazes in Caprock Canyons State Park near Quitaque, about one hundred miles southeast of Amarillo. Said to be one of the purest strains of American bison remaining in the world today, the animals have a remarkable story of survival.

That tale starts in Palo Duro Canyon, where Charles Goodnight and his partner, John Adair, established the JA Ranch. In 1876 Goodnight and his cowboys had to shoo thousands of bison out of the canyon to make room for their cattle. By 1878 he no longer had to chase the bison off. The buffalo hunters had taken care of that.

Goodnight's wife, Mary Ann, was concerned about the number of bison being slaughtered and urged her husband to save what he could from the remnants of the Southern Plains herd in the northern Texas Panhandle.

He did, by first roping a few calves and then acquiring a few others. His initial herd of five to seven animals grew to thirteen by 1887 and reached a peak of more than two hundred in the 1920s. Those animals would form one of five foundation herds from which the majority of today's herds have developed.

Thinking to preserve these shaggy symbols of the American West in a setting accessible to visitors, the Texas Parks and Wildlife Department accepted the donation of the JA's historic herd in the 1990s and moved it to Caprock Canyons in 1997. The bison, commonly called buffalo, now have the run of much of the 15,313-acre state park where the high plains of the Panhandle meet the rolling plains to the east, the landscape where millions of the bison's ancestors once roamed. Interestingly, Caprock Canyons was once part of the JA Ranch, so in a sense the bison have come back home.

Caprock Canyons State Park and Trailway | PO Box 204 | Quitaque, TX 79255
(806) 455-1492 | tpwd.state.tx.us/spdest/findadest/parks/caprock_canyons

CADDO LAKE

Caddo Indian legend says that Caddo Lake in east Texas was formed by a giant flood. Scientists agree but explain that the floodwaters backed up into the Cypress Bayou watershed when they were blocked by massive logjams on the Red River.

At any rate Caddo Lake is the only natural lake in Texas and the largest natural lake in the South. It was artificially dammed in the early 1900s, and in 1971 a new dam replaced the old one. Caddo Lake today covers 26,810 acres of cypress swamp with an average depth of only eight to ten feet. It is fed by Big Cypress Bayou and begins at Karnack, Texas, at the lake's western edge. Deeper water in the bayou averages about twenty feet.

Still in use at Caddo Lake State Park, fifteen miles northeast of Marshall, are quaint cabins built by the Civilian Conservation Corps in the 1930s. There is also a CCC pavilion. The lake itself is noted for thick stands of bald cypress (one of the largest cypress forests in the world) and the tangle of aquatic plants that thrive in its nooks and crannies.

Some come to Caddo Lake for the fishing—largemouth, sand, and yellow bass; catfish; bream; bluegill; red ear sunfish; chain pickerel—but most come for the sightseeing. Guides take visitors on aquatic tours through the maze of cypress-lined bayous and sloughs that define much of the lake, making it a magical and mysterious place. The more adventuresome may want to tour at night, when they can see an alligator or two and feel the lake's primordial spooky vibes among the moss-draped cypress groves and lush vegetation.

The relatively new Caddo Lake National Wildlife Refuge welcomes birds and birders. It was established in October 2000 for managing migratory bird and other fish and wildlife populations. Some claim they have even seen a Texas Bigfoot in the area.

Caddo Lake State Park | 245 Park Road 2 | Karnack, TX 75661
(903) 679-3351 | tpwd.state.tx.us/spdest/findadest/parks/caddo_lake

CADILLAC RANCH

Eccentric entrepreneur Stanley Marsh 3 (he always said he thought the Roman numeral III was pretentious) installed a Panhandle pop art shrine in 1974. His Cadillac Ranch was the result of Marsh's challenge to the Ant Farm, a San Francisco design collective, to create a unique work on Marsh's ranch west of Amarillo.

Said to represent the golden age of American automobiles and the rise and fall of the tailfin, ten vintage Cadillacs are half buried, fin ends up, facing west (some say at the angle of the Great Pyramid of Giza) in a cow pasture bordered by Interstate 40. They range from a 1949 club coupe to a 1963 sedan.

In 1997 Marsh moved the Cadillac Ranch a couple miles farther west from its original location to steer clear of increasing urban sprawl, because "the girls," as he called the cars, "didn't like the smell of the city. They like the fragrance of cow manure and wheat and new-broken sod." Noted for his tongue-in-cheek humor, he left the ten huge holes at the first site and erected a large sign: UNMARKED GRAVES FOR SALE OR RENT.

Over the years the original pastel colors or shiny silver of the cars—most acquired used for an average of $200 apiece—have been covered over with spray-painted graffiti. Vandals and souvenir hunters have further altered the Caddies by smashing windows and removing chrome, radios, speakers, and doors.

Marsh seemed to be okay with all that, satisfied that the installation is a public sculpture. "We think it looks better every year," he said. Nevertheless, the wheels are now welded to the axles to discourage thieves.

Visible from the highway, the Cadillac Ranch is located on private land but is definitely open to the public. The gate is always unlocked.

Cadillac Ranch, west of Amarillo, just off I-40 between exits 60 and 62

CHUCK WAGON

Originally Texas tailgating took place at the back of a wagon—a chuck wagon, to be precise. It evolved from those wagons that held food and cooking equipment as part of the wagon trains that carried settlers across the prairies, but it got its name and its efficient design in Texas.

Rancher Charles Goodnight gets credit for inventing the chuck wagon in 1866. (*Chuck* is cowboy slang for food.) He designed it to keep his cowboys fed on cattle drives as they moved longhorns up the trail to markets in New Mexico, Colorado, and Kansas. The wagon would travel ahead of the herd so the cook (or "Cookie," as he was generally called) could set up camp and have a hot meal ready by the time the trail hands arrived with the cattle.

Goodnight's first rolling kitchen was built on an army surplus Studebaker wagon he custom fitted with a sloping chuck box on the back. Built into the box were shelves and drawers to store what the cook would need in the way of utensils and easy-to-preserve staples, such as dried beans and peas, salted meat, coffee, flour, cornmeal, and starter for sourdough biscuits. A hinged lid on the front of the box folded down to make a worktable.

Chuck wagons are still around—and not just in museums. These days camp cooks set up on recreational trail rides and at outdoor festivals rather than on cattle drives. They still bake biscuits and cobbler in cast-iron Dutch ovens with rimmed lids that will hold live coals heaped on top to provide heat from above as well as from the fire below.

Today those sampling Cookie's fare are very often doing so during a chuck-wagon cook-off in which modern-day camp cooks are vying for top prize for their meats (often chicken-fried steak), beans (pinto), bread (sourdough, especially), dessert (usually cobbler and most often peach), and potatoes.

These days there are even a few professional chuck-wagon racing circuits. The events are generally part of a rodeo and require that the wagons race in a figure-eight pattern around barrels. It's likely that old-time cookies and cowboys like Charles Goodnight would think that is just downright silly.

Llano River Chuck Wagon Cook-Off | Badu Park | Llano, TX 78643
llanochuckwagoncookoff.com

COUNTY COURTHOUSES

Texans love their courthouses, all 254 of them, and some of the buildings have real architectural significance. In fact, the Lone Star State's courthouses may be unmatched in diversity and quality of design.

The most impressive ones were built during the golden age of Texas courthouses: the late 1870s through the turn of the twentieth century. With their towers, turrets, and domes, they are visual knockouts, and many are still in use today.

In some regions, the courthouse may be the only stone building, and it's likely to be the tallest and most substantial structure in the county as well. Especially on the flat plains, the courthouse is visible for miles and serves as a navigation point. Traditionally the courthouse square has been a focal point for celebrations, markets, parades, and other public functions.

Yet, over time, some of even the most spectacular structures began to fall into disrepair. By the early 1970s more than two dozen historic Texas courthouses had been destroyed. By 1998 the rest were listed among America's Most Endangered Historic Places.

So in 1999 then-governor George W. Bush and the Texas Legislature established the Texas Historic Courthouse Preservation Program, which allocates government funds to restore and preserve these architectural and historical treasures.

Among those faithfully returned to their former glory are the Erath County Courthouse in Stephenville, built in 1892, and the Ellis County Courthouse in Waxahachie, constructed in 1897. The clock tower and turrets built as part of the original 1894 Goliad Courthouse, destroyed in a 1942 hurricane, were finally replaced in 2003.

Certainly one of the most noteworthy restorations is the one in Hillsboro. The three-story Hill County Courthouse was built in 1890 and was gutted by fire in 1993. All that remained were its limestone walls and iron staircases. The county residents and elected officials rallied and saw to it that the courthouse was rebuilt by the end of the 1990s, including the seventy-foot-tall clock tower that is covered with ornate tinwork.

The work goes on.

Ellis County Courthouse | 101 W. Main St. | Waxahachie, TX 75165

Erath County Courthouse | 100 W. Washington St. | Stephenville, TX 76401

Goliad County Courthouse | North Courthouse St. | Goliad, TX 77963

Hill County Courthouse | 1 N. Waco St. | Hillsboro, TX 76645

COWBOYS

Real Texas cowboys are not urban. Nor do they wear rhinestones. Unlike their movie counterparts, they seldom use guns or sing, although some do write cowboy poetry. They are working men defined by the work they do—common men in an uncommon profession.

The techniques and tools of their trade they inherited from the Mexican *vaqueros* from south of the border, and the heyday of the cowboy on horseback began right after the Civil War. That's when enterprising Texans joined in "making the gather." They began rounding up the unbranded maverick cattle that had roamed free while men were fighting away from home during the war years.

That ushered in the period of the trail drives to get the cattle to market, lasting roughly from 1866 to about 1890. Many of the cowboys back then really were boys, oftentimes no more than eighteen or twenty years old.

Roughly one in three was Mexican or African American, and some were actually cowgirls disguising themselves as boys.

Even now an integral part of the American myth, cowboys these days still have a weakness for horses and still work cattle mostly, although the days of chasing after half-wild longhorns are long gone.

The modern-day cowboy likely spends more time in a pickup than on a horse. He may even work cattle with a four-wheeler or round 'em up with a helicopter. He studies animal nutrition, genetics, range management, and artificial insemination—subjects his forebears hadn't even heard of.

In the rodeo world the word *cowboy* can be a verb as well as a noun. To "cowboy up" means to take courage, to go ahead and tackle the job, to make the ride despite the risk. That may just sum up the iconic cowboy code in general as the mystique lives on.

Texas Cowboy Hall of Fame | 128 E. Exchange Ave. | Historic Barn A
Fort Worth, TX 76164 | (817) 626-7131 | texascowboyhalloffame.org

COYOTES

As the song says, "The coyotes wail along the trail. Deep in the heart of Texas." Actually, they yip and howl all over Texas, adaptable and opportunistic as they are. The ultimate survivors, they have slowly filled the void left by the declining population of wolves in the wild. In fact, coyotes are sometimes called "prairie wolves," and they are the most frequently viewed large carnivore in Texas.

About the size of a small German shepherd, a coyote (*Canis latrans*) weighs an average of about thirty pounds. Its coat is usually gray or buff in color, and it has a bushy tail with a black tip and fairly large ears held erect. Its legs are long and slender, and when it runs, it characteristically carries its tail down rather than horizontally like foxes or up like wolves and dogs. To note its most distinguishing feature, one must look it in the eye. A coyote's eyes are yellow with black, round pupils.

Extremely intelligent and blessed with keen senses of hearing, sight, and smell, the coyote does most of its hunting at night or early in the morning. It will eat just about anything but seems to prefer rabbits, rodents, and insects.

When a mama coyote dens up and gives birth to her babies—typically five to seven pups in a litter—the daddy coyote brings home food but is not allowed in the den. Nevertheless, coyotes are pretty much monogamous, with pairs remaining together for years—although not necessarily for life.

Coyotes rarely dig their own dens, preferring to take over one dug by a badger or to seek shelter in natural cavities. They will, of course, make necessary renovations and excavate multiple escape tunnels, as needed.

Over the years the coyote's wiliness has made it a favorite folktale trickster in the lore of Texas and the rest of the Southwest.

Texas Zoo | 110 Memorial Dr. | Victoria, TX 77901 | (361) 573-7681 | texaszoo.org

DEALEY PLAZA

What started out as a site marking the birthplace of Dallas, originally founded by John Neely Bryan in the 1840s, is now an internationally recognized murder site. Dealey Plaza, named for George Bannerman Dealey, a Dallas civic leader, was once hailed as the "Front Door of Dallas," serving as a major gateway to the city from the west end and a symbol of civic pride.

That all changed following the tragic events that took place on November 22, 1963, when alleged assassin Lee Harvey Oswald shot and killed President John F. Kennedy and wounded Texas Governor John Connally from the sixth floor of a nearby redbrick building then known as the Texas School Book Depository. Almost immediately, grief-stricken citizens began bringing flowers and mementos to Dealey Plaza, transforming it into an unofficial memorial site.

In 1993, thirty years after the assassination, Dealey Plaza was designated as a National Historic Landmark District. Meanwhile, the Sixth Floor Museum opened in 1989 in the old book depository warehouse, known today as the Dallas County Administration Building at Elm and Houston Streets in the West End Historical District of downtown Dallas. The museum chronicles President Kennedy's assassination and legacy and actually takes up two floors, the sixth and seventh.

The historical exhibition on the sixth floor includes the two evidentiary areas—the so-called sniper's nest from which the gunman fired and the corner where the rifle that fired the shots was found—restored to their 1963 appearance. The exhibition and the audio guide use historic television and radio broadcasts, films, photographs, and artifacts to tell the story of that fateful November day.

The museum also has a collection of close to eight hundred oral history interviews. The seventh-floor gallery opened in 2002 and is used for special exhibitions, events, and other public programming.

As part of the complex, the John F. Kennedy Memorial Plaza was dedicated in 1970. An aesthetically simple memorial structure in the plaza is designed as a cenotaph, or open tomb, with only three words carved into a granite square inside a roofless room: JOHN FITZGERALD KENNEDY.

Sixth Floor Museum at Dealey Plaza
411 Elm St. | *Dallas, TX 75202* | *(214) 747-6660* | *jfk.org*

DINOSAURS

Over a hundred million years ago, creatures of the early Cretaceous period trudged across inlet bays, tidal lagoons, and salt marshes in what is now north-central Texas. Their feet sank in fine-grained, limy mud and left impressions that would eventually harden and then be buried under layers of sediment.

Nowadays that same part of Texas features cedar-clad hills and limestone valleys and the

Paluxy River with such towns as Glen Rose nearby. Time and erosion over the eons eventually revealed some of the best-preserved and most numerous dinosaur fossil footprints in Texas and the world.

They were first discovered in 1909 by a schoolboy, George Adams, tramping along Wheeler Branch, a tributary of the Paluxy River. He saw a trail of large, three-toed, birdlike prints that led through the limestone streambed, and he told his Glen Rose School principal about them. The principal declared a field day the next day so the entire student body could go have a look.

Newspapers reported the find; Smithsonian paleontologists confirmed they were dinosaur tracks; and tourists, scientists, and entrepreneurs began to come. In the Depression-era 1930s, some Glen Rose–area farmers excavated and sold some of the tracks. In 1940 a rock slab containing two kinds of tracks was quarried from the Paluxy River and is now on display at Texas Memorial Museum, the exhibit hall of the Texas Natural Science Center at the University of Texas in Austin.

Local efforts to protect the dinosaur tracks in Somervell County led to the dedication of Dinosaur Valley State Park in 1970. Located about four miles west of Glen Rose,

it encompasses 1,590 acres and allows visitors to see the tracks firsthand. The best viewing is during dry weather when the Paluxy River is low, so it's a good idea to call ahead to check on river conditions. Paleontologists say the likely theropod (three-toed) track maker was *Acrocanthosaurus*, an imposing carnivore up to thirty feet long and weighing two to three tons. It was bipedal and had menacing claws, serrated teeth, and a bony ridge that ran the length of its spine.

Full-scale replicas of the dinosaurs stand in the park.

Dinosaur Valley State Park | PO Box 396 | Glen Rose, TX 76043 | (254) 897-4588
tpwd.state.tx.us/spdest/findadest/parks/dinosaur_valley

Texas Memorial Museum | 2400 Trinity St. | Austin, TX 78705
(512) 471-1604 | utexas.edu/tmm

J. FRANK DOBIE

When he was foreman of his uncle's sprawling ranch in La Salle County, J. Frank Dobie spent a lot of time listening to tales told around the campfire by an old vaquero. Those, Dobie realized, were "the tales of my folk and my land" and he began to collect them.

Dobie started out as a professional educator, first as headmaster and teacher at a high school in Alpine and then as an English teacher at his alma mater in Georgetown, Texas, Southwestern University. Later he would teach at the University of Texas, taking a year's break to work at the ranch.

That's when he heard the old vaquero's stories and realized they needed to be preserved. He believed those stories of ghost bulls, buried treasure, and clever coyotes had in them as much universal appeal as the literature from England or New England, and he began advocating for and teaching folklore from the Southwest. He rejoined the faculty at UT and then chaired the English department at what was then Oklahoma A&M University in Stillwater.

All this time Dobie was writing and publishing his stories in magazines and book collections. He had been a member of the Texas

PHILOSOPHERS' ROCK

Folklore Society since 1914 and became its secretary in 1922, beginning a program for publication. He held the post of secretary-editor of the society for twenty-one years.

His own works number close to thirty and span a fifty-seven-year period, some of them published posthumously. Never far from his rural roots, he owned a couple of ranches, the second of which was a 264-acre spread on Barton Creek, fourteen miles southwest of Austin. He called it Paisano after his personal totem, the roadrunner. It was his retreat until his death in 1964 at age seventy-five.

Paisano has been preserved and maintained, under the auspices of the University of Texas, as a writer's retreat, enabling talented writers with a Texas connection to spend six months living at the ranch, supported by a Dobie Paisano Fellowship stipend.

Dobie and his writer friends Roy Bedicheck and Walter Prescott Webb are captured in bronze outside the entrance to Barton Springs Pool in Austin in a piece of public art called *Philosophers' Rock*.

Philosophers' Rock | Barton Springs Pool | 2101 Barton Springs Rd. | Austin, TX 78704
(512) 867-3080 | ci.austin.tx.us/parks/bartonsprings.htm

DR PEPPER

Any Texan with an ounce of state pride will order a Dr Pepper over a Coca-Cola or a Pepsi any day. That's because in the soft-drink world Dr Pepper is a Texas original.

Although once rumored to be made from prune juice, Dr Pepper is actually a blend of twenty-three flavors, and that's as much as anyone is telling. Only three people know the secret formula, one of the oldest and best-kept secrets in the country, and, yes, the formula is kept in a vault at the company headquarters in Plano.

Dr Pepper's history began in Waco at Morrison's Old Corner Drug Store, where pharmacist Charles Alderton first developed the drink in 1885. It had no name back then. Customers would simply call out, "Shoot me a Waco!" It was Alderton's boss, Wade Morrison, who named the drink to honor the father of a girl he had loved or his first employer, depending on which version one hears and chooses to believe. For some reason the period after *Dr* was dropped in the 1950s.

At first the new drink was blended as a syrup and shipped to area drugstores to be individually mixed with carbonated water and served at soda fountains. Customers liked the fruity concoction well enough to increase demand, and Sam Prim in Dublin became the first bottler of Dr Pepper in 1891.

The new drink gained national exposure when it was introduced—along with hamburger and hot dog buns and ice-cream cones—to twenty million people attending the 1904 World's Fair and Exposition in St. Louis, Missouri. Since then its popularity has grown to the point that it is one of the top three soft drinks in the United States and the number-one non-cola.

Waco has a museum featuring Dr Pepper memorabilia, as does a second, older museum in Dublin.

drpeppermuseum.com

42

ENCHANTED ROCK

One of the best hikes in Texas is up a lump of pink rock—a big lump of pink rock eighteen miles north of Fredericksburg. It's called Enchanted Rock, and it is designated as a state natural area.

Technically the rock is a batholith or exfoliation dome. That is, it was first an underground formation created by a mass of molten magma that rose up to rest just below the earth's surface. At least partially uncovered by erosion now, it is the second-largest such geological formation in the United States—the other being Stone Mountain in Georgia.

The Tonkawa Indians claimed to hear cries of dead men in the rock, which seemed to creak and groan. Geologists say it simply grinds against itself as it heats and cools, producing the sometimes eerie sounds. The Apache and Comanche thought it the home of gods or spirits and came for vision quests. So the enchanted part comes from those early Native American legends.

Rising 425 feet aboveground and covering 640 acres, the pink granite dome is a commanding landmark in the 1,643-acre Enchanted Rock State Natural Area. Impressive as it is, however, the exposed dome is but the tip of the batholith. The remaining underground mass covers ninety square miles.

Visitors can reach the top of Enchanted Rock by one of two trails. The shorter and quicker one is the popular Summit Trail. It is only 0.6 mile long but does call for a fairly steady 425-foot climb. The Loop Trail is longer but gentler. Its circular four-mile path passes around most of the granite peaks.

Since Enchanted Rock is not really on the road to anywhere, it's a good idea to call ahead to make sure it's open. The park closes when it reaches capacity (in terms of parking). As the Texas Parks and Wildlife Department explains, that is one way to protect the area from overuse.

Enchanted Rock State Natural Area | 16710 Ranch Rd. 965 | Fredericksburg, TX 78624
(830) 685-3636 | tpwd.state.tx.us/spdest/findadest/parks/enchanted_rock

FORT WORTH STOCKYARDS

Fort Worth has been known as Cowtown since the post–Civil War days, when drovers headed longhorn cattle up the Chisholm Trail to the railheads farther north. Between 1866 and 1890 more than four million head of cattle were trailed through what was the last major stop for rest and supplies before crossing the Red River into Indian Territory.

Keeping the Wild West alive today is the Fort Worth Stockyards National Historic District, on the north side of town, home now to saloons, steak houses, western-wear stores, galleries, gift shops, and a hotel. No longer are diners limited to beans and biscuits, as the cowboys often were. Nowadays menus offer "urban western" fare, such as rabbit-rattlesnake sausage.

When the Texas and Pacific Railroad arrived in 1876, Fort Worth became a major cattle-shipping point, leading to the construction of the Union Stockyards by 1889. The subsequent opening of various meatpacking companies led to Fort Worth's becoming one of the country's major beef suppliers.

All that ended in the 1960s when the Swift and Armour companies closed their doors, leaving the Stockyards area as a prime candidate for renovation. It emerged as one of the most famous and entertaining historic sites in Texas.

In the heart of the Stockyards district is the mission revival–style Livestock Exchange Building, completed in 1903 and used for cattle auctions until 1992. It now houses the North Fort Worth Historical Society's museum.

Nearby is Cowtown Coliseum, site of the first indoor rodeo. It was built in 1908 to provide a permanent home for the Fort Worth Fat Stock Show and later became a performance venue for superstars such as Elvis Presley.

The cows in Cowtown are now limited to a small herd of ten to fifteen longhorns driven twice daily down Exchange Avenue by mounted cowboys. It's a token gesture, to be sure, but the longhorns don't seem to mind.

Fort Worth Stockyards | 130 E. Exchange Ave. | Fort Worth, TX 76164
(817) 624-4741 | fortworthstockyards.org

BUDDY HOLLY

One of the first songs John Lennon learned to play was "That'll Be the Day" by Buddy Holly, and the story is that Lennon and Paul McCartney decided to call their group the Beatles after Holly's band, the Crickets. Holly influenced not only the lads from Liverpool, England, but countless other young rock-and-rollers in the 1950s as well.

Born in Lubbock on September 7, 1936, he was named Charles Hardin Holley (after the e in his last name was dropped accidentally in a contract years later, he decided to leave it off). His mother thought Charles Hardin was too much name for such a little baby, so she started calling him Buddy. And Buddy he remained.

Holly recorded more than one hundred songs during his brief career, including hits such as "Peggy Sue" and "That'll Be the Day." But he was distinguished by more than song lyrics and guitar licks. His black horn-rimmed glasses and three-button Ivy League jackets made him look more

like a geek than a rock star. No one seemed to care, though, as long as he made cool music.

In 1959 Holly died in a plane crash on his way to Fargo, North Dakota, after finishing a concert in Clear Lake, Iowa. He was twenty-two.

His memory and his status as a rock-and-roll legend are assured, however, particularly in his hometown. Lubbock has a park bearing his name, the Buddy Holly Walk of Fame, and the Buddy Holly Center, located in the historic Fort Worth and Denver Railroad Depot. There is also a larger-than-life-size statue of the bespectacled musician playing his Fender Stratocaster guitar.

He was the subject of a long-running Broadway hit musical, *Buddy . . . the Buddy Holly Story*, and for folk singer Don McLean's "American Pie," an eight-minute, thirty-three-second tribute to "the day the music died."

His glasses, his guitar, and other memorabilia are now on display in the Buddy Holly Exhibition in the Buddy Holly Center in Lubbock.

Buddy Holly Center | *1801 Crickets Ave.* | *Lubbock, TX 79401*
(806) 775-3560 | *buddyhollycenter.org*

SAM HOUSTON

Texas hero Sam Houston truly has become larger than life in Huntsville, where he spent his last years. He stood six feet, two inches when he was nineteen and, some say, grew to be six feet six inches by the time he died at age seventy in 1863. But the statue honoring him in Huntsville is ten times taller: sixty-seven feet high, the world's largest statue of any American hero.

Huntsville native David Adickes created the giant likeness out of sixty thousand pounds of concrete and steel. It is visible from northbound Interstate 45 for nearly seven miles.

Even though it is the city of Houston that is named for him, he chose to settle down in Huntsville at the end of his political career, and there is no forgetting his presence in the area. There is Sam Houston University, for starters, and nearby is Sam Houston National Forest. Lake Raven uses the name given to Houston by the Cherokees.

Houston arrived in Texas, by way of Virginia and Tennessee, just in time to become a key figure in its history. A signer of the Texas Declaration of Independence, he was made commander-in-chief of the Texan forces. He led the troops that finally defeated Santa Anna at the Battle of San Jacinto on April 21, 1836, assuring Texas its independence from Mexico.

Twice president of the new Republic of Texas, he was later a US senator and governor when Texas became a state.

He is the only person to have served as governor of two states: Tennessee and Texas.

In March 1861, however, he was evicted from the Texas governorship for refusing to take an oath of loyalty to the Confederacy.

So he simply went home to Huntsville and lived in retirement with his third wife, Margaret Lea. He claimed the hills in the area reminded him of his boyhood home in Tennessee. He died of pneumonia on July 26, 1863, and is buried in Huntsville's Oakwood Cemetery.

Sam Houston Statue and Visitors Center
7600 Hwy. 75 South | Huntsville, TX 77340 | (936) 291-9726 | huntsvilletexas.com

LYNDON BAINES JOHNSON

Three US presidents have claimed residence in Texas, but only one was a true native son. The other two were born Yankees and just got to Texas as fast as they could.

The nation's thirty-sixth president, Lyndon Baines Johnson, was born near Johnson City (named for his family) and had a ranch near Stonewall in central Texas. During their sojourn in Washington, DC, the president and his wife, Lady Bird, retreated to the Texas White House at the ranch. Both are buried at the Johnson Family Cemetery there.

In his will Johnson donated the LBJ Ranch to the public, stipulating that it must be a working ranch and not "a sterile relic of the past." So white-faced Hereford cattle still graze in the pastures alongside the Pedernales River.

The ranch is now under the umbrella of the Lyndon B. Johnson National Historical Park, headquartered in Johnson City. The Lyndon B. Johnson State Park sits adjacent to the ranch and serves as a gateway to it.

In nearby Austin the Lyndon Baines Johnson Library and Museum on the University of Texas campus is the most visited presidential library in the nation, perhaps because it has modest entrance fees and free admission on eight specified days of the year in keeping with Johnson's stipulation that it "be available to all."

labor." His ambitious agenda included aid to education, attack on disease, Medicare, urban renewal, beautification, conservation, development of depressed regions, a wide-scale fight against poverty, control and prevention of crime and delinquency, and removal of obstacles to the right to vote.

The space program continued to have spectacular successes under Johnson, but there was controversy about the US involvement in Vietnam. Johnson startled the world by withdrawing as a candidate for reelection, saying he would devote his full efforts, unimpeded by politics, to the quest for peace.

During his presidency LBJ urged the nation "to build a great society, a place where the meaning of man's life matches the marvels of man's

He died suddenly of a heart attack at his Texas ranch on January 22, 1973.

Lyndon B. Johnson National Historical Park
PO Box 329 | Johnson City, TX 78636 | (830) 868-7128 | nps.gov/lyjo

Lyndon B. Johnson State Park and Historic Site | PO Box 238 | Stonewall, TX 78671
(830) 644-2252 | tpwd.state.tx.us/spdest/findadest/parks/lyndon_b_johnson

Lyndon Baines Johnson Library and Museum
2313 Red River St. | Austin, TX 78705 | (512) 721-0200 | lbjlibrary.org

JOHNSON SPACE CENTER

When Neil Armstrong and Buzz Aldrin set foot on the moon on July 20, 1969, their "giant leap for mankind" was made possible in part by Houston's own Johnson Space Center. Well, to be precise, it's Clear Lake's own Johnson Space Center, and it was still called the Manned Space Center back then.

Even before that historic Apollo mission, the site had provided mission control for the earlier Mercury and Gemini projects and succeeding space flights from the time the National Aeronautics and Space Administration got it up and running in 1965. NASA picked the southeast Harris County location out of twenty candidates investigated by a site survey team in 1961. Of course, it didn't hurt that Texas native Lyndon B. Johnson was vice president at the time.

It became NASA's hub for astronaut training and the home of Mission Control, and in 1973, the year of LBJ's death, the facility was renamed for him. It is one of nine NASA field installations and home base for the nation's astronauts.

It has three mission-control centers, one of which is in constant operation monitoring the International Space Station, the Earth-orbiting research facility constructed and manned cooperatively by NASA, the European Space Agency, and the space agencies of several other nations.

Another mission-control center, most recently manned to monitor space shuttle flights, is now used for training future controllers for the International Space Station. The third is Apollo Mission Control, now a National Historic Landmark. No longer operational, it once monitored the Mercury, Gemini, and Apollo missions, including *Apollo 13*.

Who can forget that dramatic flight signaled by "Houston, we've had a problem here," uttered when the spacecraft survived an explosion in 1970? With help from those on the ground, the crippled command module made it back to Earth with only fifteen minutes of power to spare.

The Johnson Space Center's campus has about one hundred buildings stretching across 1,620 acres. Public access to the site is limited for security reasons, but the Space Center Houston opened in 1992 to offer visitors hands-on experiences and space-themed exhibits.

Space Center Houston | 1601 NASA Pkwy.
Houston, TX 77058 | (281) 244-2100 | spacecenter.org

BARBARA JORDAN

As Barbara Jordan was growing up in Houston's Fifth Ward, her maternal grandfather had her commit to memory the idea that "the world is not a playground, but a schoolroom. Life is not a holiday but an education." She held that thought as she first pursued her education at Texas Southern University and then got a law degree at Boston University.

Still, her road to recognition as elder statesman in Texas was neither fast nor easy. As she was quick to point out, she began her political career as a "stamper and addresser" of envelopes when she volunteered during John F. Kennedy's campaign for president in 1960.

She ran unsuccessfully twice for the Texas State Senate before finally winning a seat in 1966. That victory started a string of firsts: first African American to serve in the Texas Senate since Reconstruction; first African-American woman from the South to serve in Congress; first woman and first African American to give the keynote speech at a Democratic National Convention; first African-American woman interred in the Texas State Cemetery. And yet, she said, she was not striving for firsts; she was striving for excellence.

It was her eloquence that was most impressive. She spoke with dignity, gravity, and flawless elocution in a voice both rich and resonant. The whole nation first heard her during televised remarks by members of the House Judiciary Committee making the case for or against impeachment of President Richard Nixon in the Watergate hearings. Hers was a voice of clarity on the constitutional issues at play.

As Democratic National Convention keynoter she nominated both Jimmy Carter and Bill Clinton as candidates for president. Clinton awarded her the Presidential Medal of Freedom in 1994.

She finished her career as a professor at the Lyndon B. Johnson School of Public Affairs at the University of Texas in Austin. She died in 1996.

Barbara Jordan Statue | University of Texas | Battle Oaks at Twenty-fourth St. and Whitis Ave. Austin, TX 78712 | utexas.edu/diversity/barbarajordan

Barbara Jordan Memorial Statue | Barbara Jordan Terminal Austin-Bergstrom International Airport | 3600 Presidential Blvd. | Austin, TX 78719 ci.austin.tx.us/austinairport/bjmemproject.htm

BARBARA JORDAN

KERRVILLE FOLK FESTIVAL

Regulars at the Kerrville Folk Festival—some of whom have been coming to the annual event since it started in 1972—are called Kerr-verts. Newcomers are referred to as Kerr-virgins. Although it started out indoors, the festival soon outgrew the Kerrville Municipal Auditorium, so founder Rod Kennedy bought a fifty-acre spread he calls Quiet Valley Ranch and moved the festival outdoors. Since then it's doubtful that the valley has been all that quiet during the festival's eighteen-day run. The ranch is located nine miles south of Kerrville.

The largest and longest-running festival of its kind in the United States, it celebrates singer/songwriters and offers more than one hundred acts. Some are emerging artists; others are well known. Over the years such folk music greats as Peter, Paul, and Mary and National Fiddling Champion Dick Barrett have performed. Other performers have included Willie Nelson, Lyle Lovett, Nanci Griffith, and Lucinda Williams, who introduced a country flavor to the music. The common thread is that they are all songwriters as well as performers.

Many of the thirty thousand–plus fans who show up each year choose to stay at the twenty-acre campground on the ranch, where impromptu songfests have become a festival trademark. After the last act has finished onstage, the jam sessions begin around the campfires that dot the area. Kerr-verts say it's like a family reunion.

The festival begins each year the Thursday before Memorial Day, its main stage set on a natural hillside. Attendees often bring their own chairs or blankets and set up on a grassy spot, somewhat reminiscent of the folk music gatherings of the 1960s. One might even see the occasional tie-dyed shirt in the crowd.

In November 2008 the Kerrville Folk Festival and Kerrville Wine & Music Festival (with its own "Little Folk" event hosted at the ranch over Labor Day weekend) were acquired by the nonprofit Texas Folk Music Foundation with the continuing mission "to support and promote songwriters, songwriting, folk music education, and live performances of traditional folk, bluegrass, acoustic rock, blues, country, jazz, and Americana music."

Kerrville Folk Festival | 3876 Medina Hwy. | Kerrville, TX 78028
(830) 257-3600 | kerrvillemusic.com

KING RANCH

A spread so big it can be measured in square miles as well as acres, the King Ranch in south Texas is larger than Rhode Island. It covers roughly 1,300 square miles, or 825,000 acres, and is one of the largest privately owned ranches in the country.

Recorded on the National Register of Historic Places as the "Birthplace of American Ranching," it dates back to 1853 when a steamboat captain named Richard King camped along Santa Gertrudis Creek and saw potential for a cattle range. The now-famous Santa Gertrudis strain of beef cattle—the first new strain developed in the Western Hemisphere—later was bred at the ranch. Their descendants are still grazing there, along with Santa Cruz and longhorn cattle.

The largest cattle ranch in the United States, the King Ranch raises other livestock as well and invests in various other agricultural products. It is credited with breeding the first registered American quarter horse and the Thoroughbred stallion Assault, winner of the Triple Crown in 1946.

During the 1930s Captain King's grandson Robert Kleberg Jr. saved the ranch from being divided up and sold to pay mounting debts by negotiating one of the largest private oil leases in history. Oil money carried the ranch through drought years as well.

Nowadays the ranch has gotten into a business built around commercial hunting leases, letting thousands of outsiders into the once-private kingdom teeming with such south Texas wildlife as wild turkeys, white-tailed deer, bobwhite quail, ducks, javelinas, and feral hogs.

Daily guided tours of the ranch are available from the King Ranch Visitor Center, and pretty much everything in the nearby city of Kingsville relates in one way or another to the King Ranch, including the King Ranch Museum and the King Ranch Saddle Shop.

King Ranch Visitor Center | 2205 Hwy. 141 West | Kingsville, TX 78364
(361) 592-8055 | king-ranch.com

LONE STAR

From a symbol of defiance and independence to a show of state pride, the lone star emblem has gone through several incarnations on flags associated with Texas. It is now evident not only on the official state flag, but just about everywhere, and it accounts for Texas's nickname: the Lone Star State.

The emblem predates statehood and appeared on battle banners in the mid-1830s when the idea of independence from Mexico was gaining widespread support in Texas. It rallied Texans in a show of solidarity. After independence was declared in 1836, the first official flag of the new republic was a single star closely encircled with the letters TEXAS in a field of blue. A second "national" flag of Texas had only the star centered on a field of blue, simplifying the message that Texas was an independent nation.

Yet another flag for the republic, the familiar

flag associated with Texas today, was adopted in 1839 and carried over as the state flag when Texas joined the Union in 1845. The lone star is also on the state seal, which consists of a five-pointed star encircled with olive and live oak branches.

The Texas Flag Code assigns the following symbolism to the single, or lone, star, saying it "represents ALL of Texas and stands for our unity as one for God, State, and Country." Generally, it still suggests Texas's independent spirit as well.

Other notable representations of Texas lone stars are the ones atop the San Jacinto Monument near Houston and the thirty-five-foot-tall bronze one in front of the Bob Bullock Texas State History Museum in Austin. The one on the San Jacinto Monument, by the way, is unique in that it actually has nine points, but, viewed from any angle from the ground, it appears to have only five.

Bob Bullock Texas State History Museum | 1800 N. Congress Ave. | Austin, TX 78701
(512) 936-8746 | thestoryoftexas.com

San Jacinto Monument and Museum | 1 Monument Circle | La Porte, TX 77571
(281) 479-2421 | sanjacintomuseum.org

LONGHORNS

They're back. Texas longhorns, that is—back from near extinction.

The cattle breed of choice during the post–Civil War trail-driving days, longhorns were prized for their characteristics of longevity, fertility, resistance to disease, ease of calving, and ability to thrive on marginal pastures.

Once railroads and barbed-wire fences put a stop to the trail drives, however, the longhorns were all but phased out. Ranchers began to replace them with crossbred cattle that developed faster and were better suited to the fenced ranges.

By 1927 Texas longhorn stock had dwindled so dramatically that a couple of US Forest Service rangers rallied to save the remnant. They collected a small herd of breeding stock in south Texas and moved it to a refuge—in Oklahoma. They established another herd in another refuge—in Nebraska. Meanwhile, Sid Richardson and J. Frank Dobie gathered small herds to keep in Texas state parks.

In time, cattlemen began buying up surplus animals from these preserved herds, first as curiosities and then as beef animals again. Today's more health-conscious population is clamoring for lean beef, and that's what longhorns provide: meat that is lower in fat, cholesterol, and calories. Recognized registries for the breed include the Texas Longhorn Breeders Association of America and the International Texas Longhorn Association.

Still, perhaps most of all, longhorns continue to represent the romance of the olden days of the American West and are easily recognized by their long horns, which can extend to seven feet tip to tip. Also known for their diverse coloring, at least one burnt orange animal at a time has a steady job as Bevo, the mascot for the University of Texas in Austin.

Designated as the official large mammal of Texas, the longhorn now has a permanent place in the state, without question, and the official state longhorn herd is headquartered at Fort Griffin State Historic Site, with other portions of the herd kept at various state parks.

Fort Griffin State Historic Site | 1701 N. US 283 | Albany, TX 76430
(325) 762-3592 | visitfortgriffin.com

MISSIONS

Hoping to convert the indigenous people to Catholicism and extend Spain's foothold northward from Mexico, the Spanish government and the Catholic Church founded some three dozen missions in Texas in the seventeenth and eighteenth centuries. The first mission was built near present-day San Angelo in 1632, though nothing is left of it now except a commemorative marker.

The oldest surviving structures from the period are in Goliad, and they have been largely reconstructed. Dating back to 1749 are the Mission Espíritu Santo and Presidio La Bahía at Goliad State Park. Together they compose one of the few remaining Spanish mission/fort complexes in the Western Hemisphere. The original stone chapel inside the military fort, or presidio, has been in continuous use since the 1700s and is one of the oldest Catholic churches in the United States.

Also still in operation are the three churches just south of El Paso that make up its Mission Trail. The largest is San Elizario

Chapel, dating from 1877. (The current buildings are more recent than their 1680 foundations.) The other two are Ysleta Mission and Socorro Mission.

But probably the most famous Texas missions are in San Antonio. Chief among them is San Antonio de Valero, better known as the Alamo, but there are four others that make up

San Antonio Missions National Historical Park. Together they are the largest concentration of Catholic missions in North America.

Mission Concepción is the least altered, noted for its two bell towers and its hand-carved doors, but Mission San José is the largest and the one dubbed "Queen of the Missions." Its bell tower, glistening domed top, elaborate hand-carved facade, and ornate rose window present a magnificent view.

The missions in the park are about three miles apart, but the San Juan Capistrano and San Francisco de la Espada Missions have a greater sense of solitude and remoteness. They are near dams and *acequias* (ditches) and an aqueduct that make up a Spanish-built irrigation system still in use.

Visitor centers are located at Concepción, San José, and Espada, and all of the missions remain active Catholic parishes.

Goliad State Park and Historic Site | 108 Park Rd. 6 | Goliad, TX 77963 | (361) 645-3405
tpwd.state.tx.us/spdest/findadest/parks/goliad_and_mission_espiritu_santo

El Paso Mission Trail | epcounty.com/history/missiontrail.htm

El Paso Mission Trail Association | (915) 851-9997

San Antonio Missions National Historical Park | 2202 Roosevelt Ave. | San Antonio, TX 78210
(210) 932-1001 | nps.gov/saan

MOCKINGBIRD

"*Listen to the mockingbird;* listen to the mockingbird," the old song says, and that's easy to do in Texas because mockingbirds are practically permanent residents. Furthermore, they're quite willing to nest near houses in urban and suburban areas, and they are among the loudest and most constantly vocal of birds.

As the name implies, mockingbirds are good mimics, imitating not only the songs and calls of other birds, but also the sounds of other animals and even machines—sirens and car alarms, for example. Adopted as the state bird of Texas in 1927, the mockingbird lives up to its Latin name, *Mimus polyglottos,* meaning "many-tongued mimic." The males, especially the bachelors, sing year-round, especially through moonlit nights and in the first light of early morning. A male mockingbird may have a repertoire of fifty to two hundred songs. Females sing, too, but more quietly and less often.

Extremely territorial, the mockingbird seems to have no fear and can be very aggressive when its territory is invaded; it has been seen attacking even a rattlesnake. When any perceived predators are present, including cats and dogs, mockingbirds will dive and attack and generally harass until the intruders are no longer considered threats. Even humans may be targeted, and on occasion, a mockingbird has been known to attack its own reflection.

Generally mockingbirds subsist on insects, berries, and seeds. Both males and females are gray on top with white undersides. White patches on their wings look like bars, and they have long, black tails and long, slender beaks. While foraging, they may spread their wings in a peculiar two-step motion to display distinctive white patches. Even ornithologists aren't sure whether this behavior is part of a courting ritual, a territorial display, or simply a maneuver to startle insects out of hiding.

At any rate, mockingbirds can be loud and brash and apparently a little full of themselves—just the sort of descriptions applied to Texans in general.

Wild Texas | wildtexas.com/wildguides/mockingbird.php

NEIMAN MARCUS

Vogue magazine once described Neiman Marcus as "Texas with a French accent." The first retail store outside of New York to advertise in national fashion magazines, the upscale specialty store can hardly be described as a mom-and-pop operation. But it does have brother-and-sister origins. Herbert Marcus and his sister Carrie Marcus Neiman, plus Carrie's husband, Al, founded the Dallas store in 1907.

Herbert's oldest son, Stanley, joined the business in 1926, fresh out of Harvard with his business administration degree. He became the store's driving force. Under his guidance, Neiman Marcus expanded and premiered the first weekly fashion show in the United States.

Another of his innovative retailing ideas was the annual Christmas catalog, which grew to be especially popular with the addition of the now legendary "his-and-hers" gifts—outlandish and outlandishly expensive gifts such as vicuña coats, a pair of airplanes, submarines, "Noah's Ark" (including pairs of endangered animals), and Egyptian mummy cases. A bit of a spoof on the upscale—and maybe uppity—image of the store, these gifts were advertised for the man and woman who had everything.

A persistent urban myth is that even Neiman's chocolate chip cookie recipe is expensive. According to legend, a customer requested the recipe after sampling a cookie at the store. The waiter said there would be a "two-fifty" charge, but it turned out to be $250 and not $2.50. Although the story is untrue, Neiman Marcus has long published a cookie recipe on its website to quell the rumors and invited people to print it out and send it along to friends.

Still, from the beginning the store has had a reputation for high prices as well as high quality, prompting some disparaging customers to call it "Needless Mark-ups." Founder Herbert Marcus would no doubt argue against that label since his basic tenet was "It's never a good sale for Neiman Marcus unless it's a good buy for the customer."

The flagship store is still in downtown Dallas, but Neiman Marcus is no longer family-owned. It is a chain with more than forty stores scattered across the country. It even has outlet stores called Last Call Clearance Centers.

Neiman Marcus | 1618 Main St. | Dallas, TX 75201 | (214) 741-6911 | neimanmarcus.com

OIL WELLS

There was a time in Texas when the discovery of underground oil was considered a nuisance when drillers were really looking for water. That's before anyone knew what to do with the black stuff.

Of course, the Native Americans had known about aboveground oil seeps for centuries and had used oil to treat a variety of ailments. In the sixteenth century, Spanish explorers forced aground on the Texas Gulf coast used oil floating on the surface of the water to caulk their boats and waterproof their boots.

But it wasn't until after the Civil War that enough people were using oil products for lighting and lubrication to make it worthwhile for purposeful drilling to take place. The first producing oil well in Texas was drilled in Melrose in Nacogdoches County in 1866, and the first big producing oil field developed in Corsicana, beginning in 1894 when city workers discovered it by accident while drilling for water.

The first true boom, however, came after Anthony Lucas brought in the world's first great oil gusher on January 10, 1901, near Beaumont on Spindletop Hill. Oil spewed more than one hundred feet in the air, well above the sixty-foot-high derrick, for nine days until the well was finally capped and the oil flowed at an estimated 100,000 barrels a day.

That discovery helped usher in the liquid-fuel age that brought forth the automobile, the

EAST TEXAS OIL MUSEUM

airplane, the highway network, improved railroad and marine transportation, the era of mass production, and the country's dependence on oil.

Texas is still the largest producer of oil and natural gas (discovered as a by-product of oil) in the United States. No other state or region worldwide has been as thoroughly explored or drilled for oil or natural gas as Texas, so oil pump jacks are likely to remain fairly common sights throughout the state.

Spindletop–Gladys City Boomtown Museum
PO Box 10070 | Beaumont, TX 77710 | (409) 835-0823

East Texas Oil Museum | Hwy. 259 at Ross Street | Kilgore, TX 75662
(903) 983-8295 | easttexasoilmuseum.com

PALO DURO CANYON

Contrary to the perceptions of many, the Panhandle of Texas is not one endless, flat plain. As a matter of fact, a huge gash in the tabletop stretches from just east of the town of Canyon down toward Silverton. Encompassing 26,275 acres, it is Palo Duro Canyon, the second-largest canyon in the United States and generally called the "Grand Canyon of Texas." It is up to twenty miles wide and plunges as deep as one thousand feet.

Carved by the Prairie Dog Fork of the Red River over millions of years, the canyon was named after the Spanish for "hard wood," no doubt in reference to the abundance of mesquite and juniper trees early Spanish explorers found down in the canyon. Humans have been roaming the area for twelve thousand years, the first being nomadic tribes hunting for mammoth and giant bison.

In the 1930s the Civilian Conservation Corps built roads, a visitor center, and other buildings after the State of Texas purchased the land in the upper canyon. Palo Duro Canyon State Park officially opened on July 4, 1934. The rustic stone visitor center built by the CCC is still in use at the rim of the canyon as a museum and museum store.

In addition to the usual park activities of camping, hiking, horseback riding, bird watching, and the like, there is the popular outdoor theater production *Texas*. During the summer the musical presents glimpses of early Panhandle culture in the Pioneer Amphitheatre, with sheer canyon walls as a backdrop.

Mostly, though, the natural formations in the canyon still steal the show. They have names like the Lighthouse and the Spanish Skirts, and they continue to amaze and delight with color and form.

Artist Georgia O'Keeffe once described Palo Duro Canyon as her "spiritual home." To see it is to understand.

Palo Duro Canyon State Park | 11450 Park Rd. 5 | Canyon, TX 79015
(806) 488-2227 | palodurocanyon.com

PICKUP TRUCKS

They have been called "Texas Cadillacs," and even people who never haul anything more than groceries may well own pickup trucks in the Lone Star State. Texas is consistently the nation's leader in pickup sales. It's a cultural thing.

Automobile manufacturers have noticed. They offer special editions of their pickup trucks with names such as "Texas Edition," "Lone Star Edition," and "King Ranch." They know that in Texas bigger is better, so new designs feature bigger

engines, bigger tires (sometimes duals in the rear), and extended crew cabs that provide full backseats and four-door convenience.

There was a time when pickups were humble farm vehicles. In fact, the earliest ones were homemade modifications of Model Ts, but those days are gone. Sure, many Texans still work on farms or ranches or in oil fields, where a pickup might actually be practical and useful, but the local banker or county judge is just as likely to choose a pickup as the preferred ride. It's not just the good old boys, either; a goodly number of Texas womenfolk buy and drive pickups as well.

Generally these days the pickup of choice will probably be a high-tech model with leather-covered seats and power everything, and it must be full-size to qualify as a vehicular status symbol, even with rising gasoline prices.

Even retired or non-functioning pickups are sometimes kept and "put out to pasture" by their owners. They may literally be parked in the middle of a field to serve as hay troughs for livestock, or they may be kept around for spare parts. Sometimes the bed of a pickup may be separated from the cab and fitted out with a hitch to become a cargo trailer. Real antiques may be restored and shown as "classic" vehicles.

It's hard to say what accounts for a Texan's particular fondness for pickups. It may derive from a mythos similar to that of the horse in the American West, but in any case, it's safe to say that in Texas it is just plumb cool to own a pickup.

Texas Classic Truck and Car Shows | oldride.com/events/texas.html

QUARTER HORSE

The adjective "quarter" in American quarter horse does not imply for a moment that the breed is only 25 percent equine. No, indeed. It has to do with the horse's sprinting ability in quarter-mile races, some having been clocked at speeds up to fifty-five miles per hour. The first breed of horse native to the United States, it had its beginnings in the Virginia and Carolina colonies, where descendants of Spanish Barbs, acquired from the Chickasaws, were bred with colonial stock and used mostly for short-distance racing. When it came to Texas, however, the American quarter horse transitioned from racehorse to cow pony.

On the Texas range, American quarter horse stallions were bred with mustang mares to produce strong, agile mounts capable of enduring the harsh climate and rugged conditions on the cattle trails. Speed and strength were the principal traits cowboys required in a horse for all their gathering, roping, branding, and other chores on the open range and, later, on ranches.

A legendary lineage among prized Texas quarter horses can be traced back to a racer named Steel Dust brought to Texas from Kentucky as a yearling in 1844. In a quarter-mile match race with a local favorite in Collin County near McKinney, Steel Dust won the race and earned a reputation for speed. His descendants were prized by cowboys for use on ranches, and he became the most influential sire for the Texas strain of American quarter horse. In fact, the line became known as "steeldusts."

It was in Texas that a bunch of American quarter horse enthusiasts got themselves together in 1940 in Fort Worth. They formed the American Quarter Horse Association, now headquartered in Amarillo. The AQHA has registered more than five million American quarter horses since its inception, making it the world's largest equine breed registry and membership organization.

Said to be the most popular horse breed in the United States, the quarter horse is versatile as well. It is now bred for arena events, such as rodeo and cutting horse contests, as well as for racing and ranching.

American Quarter Horse Hall of Fame and Museum
2601 East I-40 | Amarillo, TX 79104 | (806) 376-5181 | aqha.com

RATTLESNAKES

Texans figure that with ten or eleven species or subspecies of rattlesnakes calling the Lone Star State home, they're bound to come face-to-fang with one sooner or later. At least rattlesnakes usually give fair warning before they strike.

The unmistakable low-pitched whir emanates from the reptile's tail, where shed skin forms the distinctive buttons of the rattle. It can be quite loud—up to eighty decibels—and is guaranteed to get attention.

As a rule, rattlers like to den up in dry, rocky crevices, but they also venture out to slither through grass or occasionally take a nap under a woodpile. The three species most likely to interact significantly with humans are the prairie rattler, the eastern timber or canebrake rattler, and the western diamondback.

This last is the biggest, baddest one of all, the one most willing to bite and the one that can grow to be more than seven feet long. Its scientific name is *Crotalus atrox*, with *atrox* meaning "frightful" or "grim." Mentioned often in legend and lore, it is probably the state's signature snake.

For whatever comfort this statistic might offer, annually very few people die from rattlesnake poisoning—fewer than 1 percent of those bitten. As a matter of fact, herpetologists say that bites are rare because, for the most part, the snakes are terrified of people and know they are not food.

People, on the other hand, sometimes eat rattlesnake meat—said, of course, to taste like chicken. They also save the rattles, tan the skins, or have taxidermists mount the remains of dispatched snakes. The World's Largest Rattlesnake Round-Up is hosted every year in Sweetwater, about forty miles south of Abilene. At least some hunters employ the catch-and-release method, simply relocating the snakes.

For it must be noted that the rattlers help control rodent populations and rodent-borne diseases and have their place in the overall ecological mix—something to keep in mind out on the trail.

World's Largest Rattlesnake Round-Up | *Nolan County Coliseum at Newman Park*
1699 Cypress St. | *Sweetwater, TX 79556* | *rattlesnakeroundup.net*

RIO GRANDE

Mexicans call it the Rio Bravo del Norte. Texans call it the Rio Grande. For some 1,200 miles it separates the United States from Mexico. With headwaters in the San Juan Mountains in southwestern Colorado, it enters Texas at the northwest corner of El Paso and then flows south to the Gulf of Mexico in Brownsville. It is the longest river in Texas.

The Pecos River, the Rio Conchos, and the Devils River are all tributaries. At the confluence of the Devils River and the Rio Grande, the Amistad Dam creates a reservoir near Del Rio, Texas. The name of the dam and the lake is the Spanish word for "friendship." As it curves to the northeast in a remote stretch in west Texas, it defines the 118-mile southern border of Big Bend National Park. There the Rio Grande is particularly scenic, carving its way through canyons

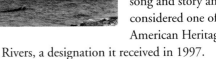

whose walls slope and seem to tilt. Sunlight glances off the walls and water. This portion of the river is designated as part of the National Wild and Scenic Rivers System.

But on the whole these days, the Rio Grande is not particularly grand, at least not in terms of size and water flow. Tremendous water use in big cities and vast irrigated acreages along the river have taken a heavy toll, reducing the river to about one-fifth of its historical discharge into the sea.

Although steamboats once operated around Brownsville and Rio Grande City, the river is now barely navigable by small boats in a few places and certainly not by oceangoing ships or even smaller passenger boats or cargo barges.

Even in its diminished state, however, the Rio Grande is still romanticized in song and story and is considered one of the American Heritage Rivers, a designation it received in 1997.

National Wild and Scenic River | Designation from river mile 842.3 above Mariscal Canyon to river mile 651.1 at the Terrell–Val Verde line | rivers.gov/wsr-rio-grandetexas.html

RUBY REDS

The state's official fruit came about as a result of an accident, so to speak.

That would be the Texas red grapefruit (*Citrus x paradisi*), marketed under the name "ruby."

In 1929 a red grapefruit was found growing on a pink grapefruit tree, and it spawned a whole industry, becoming the first grapefruit to be granted a US patent and being designated the official state fruit in 1993. Red grapefruit cultivation became an agricultural success in the Texas Rio Grande valley, and new varieties were developed to retain the red tones, even going high-tech by using radiation to trigger mutations. Texas is now the third-largest citrus grower in the United States.

The grapefruit was a hybrid in the first place, first bred in Barbados in the eighteenth century as a cross between the pomelo and the sweet orange. It was once called "the forbidden fruit" and grown as an ornamental plant. Since the late nineteenth century, however, it has been popular as an edible fruit, and the subtropical region of south Texas soon became a major producer.

With the development of the Ruby Red came real agricultural and commercial success. The distinctive Rio Red variety now has its own registered trademarks: Rio Star and Ruby-Sweet, sometimes promoted as "reddest" and "Texas choice." Texas red grapefruit is sweeter and less acidic than other grapefruit varieties, and it can boast nutritional pluses in the form of vitamin C and lycopene. The only consideration that may make it "forbidden" these days is its interaction with some drugs, especially statins.

The grapefruit gets its name, by the way, because the fruit once grew in clusters on a tree, similar in appearance to clusters of grapes on a vine. However it grows these days, to be "official" in Texas that grapefruit had better be red on the inside.

Texas Citrus Fiesta | *220 E. Ninth St.* | *Mission, TX 78572*
(956) 585-9724 | *texascitrusfiesta.net*

SAN ANTONIO RIVER WALK

In the midst of downtown San Antonio, tourists especially take sun-dappled strolls along the banks of the Paseo del Rio (River Walk) one level below the city's streets. Now celebrated as a major tourist attraction in San Antonio, which draws millions of visitors each year, the famous waterway might well have been made into a paved-over storm drain had not a group of women come to its rescue back in the 1920s.

The San Antonio Conservation Society first battled city officials and engineers who proposed straightening bends in the San Antonio River and taking out several historic buildings in the process. The women in the conservation group arranged to take the city commissioners on canoe rides to see firsthand the scenic beauty along the river's natural course. They also staged a puppet show titled *The Goose That Lays the Golden Egg* with a pretty clear moral that it would be wise to "spare this Goose [the river] for future use." The commissioners apparently got the message.

A visionary young architect, Robert H. H. Hugman, was brought in to create a world apart. At one point in the design process he envisioned a sort of Texanized version of Venice, Italy, with gondolas plying the river. No gondolas appeared, but there are river barges on which tour guides share historic tidbits and a few laughs.

The stone walkways beside the river itself connect shops, restaurants, hotels, and museums with views of historic and modern architecture and lush tropical vegetation. Sounds of mariachis serenading diners and jazz emanating from clubs and pubs complement the rhythm of voices and footsteps.

The River Walk is longer now with a new Museum Reach addition stretching north and featuring a lock and dam system—the only one in Texas—to overcome a nine-foot rise in elevation and allow passage for the river taxis. Public art installations line the banks, and the new access leads to the San Antonio Museum of Art and the historic Pearl Brewery. More development is planned both north and south of downtown.

Paseo del Rio | 110 Broadway, Suite 500 | San Antonio, TX 78205
(210) 227-4262 | thesanantonioriverwalk.com

SAN JACINTO MONUMENT

From the top of the 570-foot-high San Jacinto Monument (actually, the observation deck is only five hundred feet up), visitors can contemplate the sweep of Texas history where, after weeks of retreating, Sam Houston's rag-tag Texas army defeated Santa Anna's Mexican army on the ground below the monument in an eighteen-minute battle on April 21, 1836. An added attraction today, moored just across the coastal plains where the Texans had camped back in 1836, rests the *Battleship Texas*, which served in both world wars.

The 1,200-acre San Jacinto Battleground State Historic Site is located just minutes from downtown Houston, although its actual address is in La Porte. It was on those grounds that a force of 910 Texans took General Antonio Lopez de Santa Anna's troops by surprise attack, thereby gaining Texas its independence from Mexico and its beginning as a republic. The battle cry was "Remember the Alamo!" and the battle flag declared, LIBERTY OR DEATH.

The commemorative monument recognizing that decisive victory was begun one hundred years later in 1936 and completed in 1939. It is dedicated "to Heroes of the Battle of San Jacinto and all others who contributed to the independence of Texas." Built of limestone, the obelisk is listed as the world's tallest war memorial, fifteen feet taller than the Washington Monument in Washington, DC. The shaft itself is octagonal, forty-eight feet at its base, tapering upward to thirty feet at the observation deck and nineteen feet at the base of its crowning jewel: a thirty-four-foot, 220-ton star symbolizing the Lone Star Republic.

The foundation base is 125 feet square, with text panels highlighting significant events in history leading up to and resulting from the Texas Revolution. Within the base is the San Jacinto Museum of History, housing a collection that spans more than four hundred years of early Texas history. The museum's bronze doors carry reliefs of the six flags of Texas.

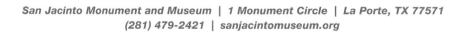

San Jacinto Monument and Museum | 1 Monument Circle | La Porte, TX 77571
(281) 479-2421 | sanjacintomuseum.org

STATE CAPITOL

Living up to its reputation of always trying to be the best and have the biggest, Texas saw to it that its state capitol in Austin is the largest in the nation, second only in square footage to its national counterpart in Washington, DC. And its dome is higher, rising almost fifteen feet above the one on the national capitol.

The current Texas State Capitol is actually the third. The first was modest indeed, built of plank lumber, and the second—a Greek revival structure—burned in late 1881. That same year an architect named Elijah E. Meyers won a nationwide competition for the design of a new capitol building. Construction began in 1882 and was completed in 1888.

Meyers first proposed using native limestone or sandstone for the exterior of the building, but the limestone streaked when exposed to air. So he suggested another native stone, pink granite. It would be more expensive, but the average Texan is game for a little horse trading. Owners of a granite quarry near Marble Falls, only about fifty miles away, agreed to donate the "sunset red" stone in exchange for a rail connection to Austin. The Austin and Northwest Railroad built an extension to carry the granite—fifteen thousand carloads of it—to the building site.

More trading ensued. In exchange for constructing the capitol, contractors were offered three million acres of land in the Texas Panhandle. This acreage would become the famous XIT Ranch.

The capitol opened to the public on San Jacinto Day, April 21, in 1888. In 1993 an underground extension to the capitol was completed to the north, and a comprehensive restoration of the original building was completed in 1995.

Sited on one of Austin's highest points, the capitol commands a sweeping view toward the Colorado River to the south, and the main campus of the University of Texas is just four blocks to the north. The capitol dome is visible from a number of vantage points around the city.

Capitol Visitors Center | 112 E. Eleventh St. | Austin, TX 78711
(512) 305-8400 | tspb.state.tx.us/SPB/capitol/texcap.htm

96

STATE FAIR

Two words pretty well sum up the State Fair of Texas: *big* and *fried*. The big part starts with Big Tex, the fifty-two-foot-tall cowboy statue that greets visitors at the fairgrounds. But he wasn't born a cowboy. He started out as Santa Claus in Kerens, Texas, southwest of Dallas, but the novelty wore off after a couple of years. So the state fair president bought the component parts for $750 and hired an artist to turn him into a giant cowboy. Big Tex made his debut at the 1952 state fair.

Then there's the Texas Star, the tallest Ferris wheel in the Western Hemisphere (but only the twenty-fifth-tallest in the history of Ferris wheels). It is 212.5 feet tall and has forty-four gondolas that will seat up to six people each. From the top of the wheel riders can see the skyline of Fort Worth almost forty miles away.

Since 1942 fairgoers have been chowing down on Fletcher's Original Corny Dogs: cornmeal-battered hot dogs served on a stick and, of course, deep-fried. Now added to the concession menus are deep-fried s'mores, fried guacamole, chicken-fried bacon, deep-fried butter, and deep-fried peaches and cream, with new high-cholesterol taste treats added every year in competition for the Big Tex Choice Award. Recent entries included deep-fried liquids: fried beer encased in a pretzel pocket, a frozen margarita morphed into a funnel cake served in a salt-rimmed glass, and lemonade in the form of a glaze on top of a lemon-flavored pastry both baked and fried. It's enough to bring on a heart attack, just thinking about it.

The largest state fair by total attendance in the United States, the State Fair of Texas in Dallas usually runs for twenty-four days, typically starting on the last Friday in September and ending sometime in October. An estimated three million or more people attend annually. It's been going on since 1886.

State Fair of Texas | Fair Park in Dallas | PO Box 150009 | Dallas, TX 75315
(214) 565-9931 | bigtex.com

SWIMMING HOLES

In the heat of a Texas summer, nothing is quite so welcome as a good old swimming hole, and the Lone Star State has a bunch to choose from.

The Hill Country in central Texas offers Krause Springs, near Spicewood, a beautiful natural pool shaded by thousand-year-old cypress trees; Hamilton Pool Preserve in southwest Travis County, with forty-five-foot waterfalls pouring over a fern-cloaked grotto; Blue Hole, tucked among tall bald cypresses in Wimberley; and Devil's Waterhole at Inks Lake State Park. The city of Austin has spring-fed Barton Springs Pool and Deep Eddy Pool, said to be the oldest swimming pool in Texas and listed as a historic landmark.

Farther west, like an oasis in the desert, the 1.75-acre pool at Balmorhea State Park is fed by millions of gallons of crystal-clear cold water bubbling up from the San Solomon Springs. It is chock-full of a variety of fish, invertebrates, and amphibians and is popular for scuba diving as well as swimming. Both the pool and the historic San Solomon Courts lodge were constructed by the Civilian Conservation Corps in the early 1930s.

Other swimming holes have been roped off or otherwise designated near the shores of various Texas lakes and rivers. Lake Fryer at Wolf Creek Park in Perryton provides a place to swim in the Panhandle, and spring-fed Burger's Lake in Fort Worth is part of a thirty-acre park. East Texas has Ratcliff Lake, tucked in the Davy Crockett National Forest. Among the river swimming holes are the deepwater pool at Brinks Crossing on the Guadalupe River in Center Point, a secluded loop on the Medina River just north of Bandera, and the constant seventy-two-degree water in the San Marcos River in San Marcos.

In all, more than two dozen more-or-less natural swimming holes are listed by the *Guide to Texas Outside,* and these are just the best-known, developed ones.

TEX-MEX

A fairly new term for an old style of cooking, Tex-Mex suggests the hybrid origins of a unique cuisine: Mexican food Texanized. The label didn't come into vogue—at least not in print—until 1973, according to the *Oxford English Dictionary*. But purveyors of Tex-Mex had been around long before it even had a name.

Pioneer providers were pushcart vendors selling chili (now the state dish), tamales, and pecan pralines in the Texas city streets of the late nineteenth century. Then came old-fashioned Mexican restaurants in the first half of the twentieth century. These establishments catered to Anglo tastes and featured combination plates with a mix of enchiladas and tacos and refried beans. By today's standards that fare was pretty bland.

By the 1970s, when the new Tex-Mex term emerged, diners wanted hotter and spicier dishes. They also were becoming more health conscious and were increasingly wary of those lard-laden combination plates. So restaurants began to offer flour tortillas, fresh salsas, and grilled meats seasoned with chili peppers.

Consider the evolution of the taco. Early on it was a one-size, crisp-fried corn tortilla shell, machine-shaped to form a *U*. It was filled with fried ground beef and topped with shredded lettuce, chopped tomatoes and onions, and shredded cheddar cheese. It's still possible to order this regulation Texas favorite, the crispy taco.

But today there are choices: crispy or soft; flat, folded, or rolled; fried in fat or heated on a griddle; made with corn or flour tortillas; filled with fajita meat, roast pork, steak, stewed chicken, sautéed mushrooms, fried fish, shrimp, avocado, and even more exotic possibilities.

Still, even with the innovations in Tex-Mex food and the addition of dishes from the interior of Mexico, there remain the familiar major Tex-Mex food groups: nachos, enchiladas, tacos, fajitas, and margaritas. And they're likely to be around for a good long while.

Joe T. Garcia's | 2201 N. Commerce St. | Fort Worth, TX 76164 | (817) 626-4356 | joets.com

Mi Tierra Café y Pandería | 218 Produce Row | San Antonio, TX 78207
(210) 225-1262 | mitierracafe.com

Fonda San Miguel | 2330 W. North Loop | Austin, TX 78756
(512) 459-4121 | fondasanmiguel.com

and many more . . .

TEXAS RANGERS

Nowadays the Texas Rangers can refer to either a baseball team or what claims to be the oldest (or at least the second-oldest) law enforcement body in North America. Without question the latter has the longer history and, arguably, the much more interesting one.

The law enforcement Texas Rangers were first put together in 1823 by Stephen F. Austin to protect his settlement from Indian raids. Texas was still part of Mexico then, and Austin got permission to form two companies of men "to act as rangers for the common defense."

In 1835, during the run-up to the Texas Revolution, the Texas Rangers became more nearly an official institution, and their numbers increased to three companies of fifty-six men each. The Rangers were the primary providers of law and order during the Republic years, from 1836 through 1845, when Texas became a state. Then General Zachary Taylor incorporated the Rangers into his troops during the Mexican War of 1846, and they gained national prominence for the first time.

For the most part, however, until well after the Civil War their mission was to guard against Indian and Mexican incursions. But by the end of the nineteenth century their responsibilities had changed from military protection to law enforcement, duties they continue to perform today as part of the Texas Department of Public Safety.

A motto of sorts—"One Riot, One Ranger"—emerged from an incident in Dallas in 1896. The story is that Ranger Captain William "Bill" McDonald was dispatched to Dallas to stop an illegal prizefight. When he stepped off the train, the mayor met him and asked where the other lawmen were. McDonald is said to have replied, "Ain't I enough? There's only one prizefight!" A large bronze statue at Love Field in Dallas honors the Rangers.

Many radio and television shows—most notably *The Lone Ranger* and *Walker, Texas Ranger*—and movies and books have spotlighted the Texas Rangers and helped add to the mystique of this unique group. In Waco the Texas Ranger Hall of Fame and Museum pays tribute to the "good guys (and now gals)," those who wear the white hats.

Texas Ranger Hall of Fame and Museum | 100 Texas Ranger Trail | Waco, TX 76706
(254) 750-8631 | texasranger.org

TEXAS STATE RAILROAD

The official railroad of Texas goes only twenty-five miles, from Rusk to Palestine or Palestine to Rusk. Boarded now for entertainment, it takes passengers through the hardwood creek bottoms of the east Texas piney woods, traveling over twenty-four bridges along the route. The trip from one vintage train depot to the other takes ninety minutes.

In the beginning, the railroad had a more utilitarian purpose. It was established in 1881 to transport hardwood to fuel the furnaces at the prison-operated iron smelter at Rusk Penitentiary. Inmates built the line in stages, from Rusk all the way to Maydelle by 1906 and finally to Palestine by 1909.

The original construction was narrow gauge but was later built in standard gauge. The standard gauge made the line accessible to the main railway lines, increasing commerce in and around the area. The prison ceased operation of the iron furnaces in 1913, and regular rail service discontinued locally in 1921.

First the Texas & New Orleans (Southern Pacific Railroad) and then the Texas Southeastern Railroad leased the line and continued operating it until 1969. It was conveyed to the Texas Parks and Wildlife Department in 1972 and became part of a state historical park, the skinniest one in Texas. In 2003 the Seventy-eighth State Legislature gave it the Official Railroad of Texas designation.

Since 2007 the railroad has been under the private management of the American Heritage Railways and is no longer part of the state park system. Its nostalgic appeal hasn't changed, however, and the train still chugs and chuffs through fragrant forests and alongside wildflower meadows and pristine lakes.

Historic steam engines still pull the passenger cars, some of them climate controlled and fitted out with linen-covered tables for a premium ride. Other enclosed cars have coach-style upholstered seating or benches and only what air conditioning windows can provide. Some diesel train excursions are offered as well.

For a price one can even ride in the engine's cab or charter the caboose.

Texas State Railroad State Historical Park | Park Rd. 76, US 84 West | Rusk, TX 75785
(888) 987-2561 | texasstaterr.com

TYLER ROSES

Tyler, Texas, is the place to go for those who want to "smell the roses."

Credit the peach blight with the rise of Tyler as the "Rose Capital of the Nation." Tyler's location in the fertile growing area in east Texas meant it had long been known for the quality of its agriculture. First cotton was the leading cash crop; then truck farming and fruit orchards became increasingly important.

By the turn of the twentieth century, there were more than a million fruit trees, mainly peach, in Tyler and the rest of Smith County. Then along came the peach blight that wiped out much of the fruit industry. So a good many farmers turned to growing roses, and the roses thrived with the fortuitous combination of sandy loam soil, year-round rainfall, and moderate climate.

By the 1920s millions of rosebushes were being grown in local fields, and the rose industry

in and around Tyler had developed into a major business. By the 1940s more than half the supply of rosebushes in the United States was grown within ten miles of Tyler.

Plants from Tyler still contribute one-fifth of the nation's field-grown rosebushes, and since 1952 Tyler has been home to the nation's largest municipal rose garden. Planted on fourteen acres, the Municipal Rose Garden has more than thirty-eight thousand bushes and more than six hundred varieties. It is one of twenty-four All-America Rose Selections test gardens and has a one-acre area devoted to antique rose varieties dating back to 1867.

Each year in October, when the garden is in full bloom, the city celebrates the rose industry with the Tyler Rose Festival, begun in 1933 at the urging of the Tyler Garden Club. Near the municipal garden is the Tyler Rose Museum, which highlights the history of the local rose industry and the rose festival.

Texas Rose Festival and Tyler Rose Museum | 420 Rose Park Dr. | Tyler, TX 75702
(903) 597-3130 | texasrosefestival.com

WILDFLOWERS

Technically, Texas has five state flowers (so far)—and they're all bluebonnets. That's because the state legislature, in a diplomatic compromise move, had to amend its original designation of only the *Lupinus subcarnosus*, "generally known as buffalo clover or bluebonnet," as the state flower and include *Lupinus texensis* "and any other variety of bluebonnet not heretofore recorded."

The whole state-flower controversy started back in 1901, when the legislators finally got around to choosing a state blossom. The National Society of Colonial Dames in America won the day with its nomination of the *Lupinus subcarnosus* bluebonnet over two other proposals: the cotton boll and the cactus bloom. (Never mind that the cotton boll is not really a flower.)

But the Bluebonnet Wars continued for seventy years after all those other varieties of bluebonnets came to light, especially the *Lupinus texensis*, which is the most prolific and popular, drawing thousands of tourists to central Texas every spring. So the legislature settled the issue by elevating any and all bluebonnets to official-flower status.

Complementing the iconic bluebonnet are other strikingly beautiful wildflowers across the state: Far west Texas has its yellow poppies spread on the foothills of the Franklin

Mountains. The Panhandle has acres of golden sunflowers and milky-white yucca blooms. The Gulf coast dunes are covered with the purple goat's foot morning glory. East Texas has a profusion of yellow coreopsis and red Indian paintbrush along the roadsides.

The biggest spring fling of all, though, is in central Texas. That's where the most bluebonnets are, mixing in a colorful display with some of those other showy blossoms. The Texas Department of Transportation plants thirty-three thousand pounds of wildflower seeds along the state's roads and highways each year.

That's part of the legacy of Lady Bird Johnson's "beautify America" campaign when her husband, Lyndon, was president of the United States. A national research center Mrs. Johnson and actress Helen Hayes founded in Austin is named in her honor: the Lady Bird Johnson Wildflower Center.

Bluebonnet Festival | Chappell Hill Historical Society
9220 Poplar St. | Chappell Hill, TX 77426 | (979) 836-6033
chappellhillmuseum.org/festivals.htm

Burnet Bluebonnet Festival | Burnet Chamber of Commerce
229 S. Pierce St. | Burnet, TX 78611 | (512) 756-4297
burnettexas.com/burnettexas-bluebonnetfestival.htm

Lady Bird Johnson Wildflower Center | 4801 La Crosse Ave. | Austin, TX 78739
(512) 232-0100 | wildflower.org

WIND FARMS

Back in the olden days, windmills in Texas were used to pump water. Some of those relics are still around and still working. But a whole new kind of wind power is in the works now, especially in west Texas and in the Panhandle, where the wind comes sweeping across the plains in steady blows and dramatic gusts.

Nowadays impressively tall towers topped by giant three-bladed turbine fans stand by the hundreds across thousands of acres, generating electrical power. The largest wind farms in the country—no, make that the world—are located in Texas, and the Lone Star State produces the most wind power of any US state.

On the stretch between Abilene and Sweetwater in Taylor and Nolan Counties the wind turbines stand thick like some installation from outer space. They give the otherwise rather barren landscape an eerie

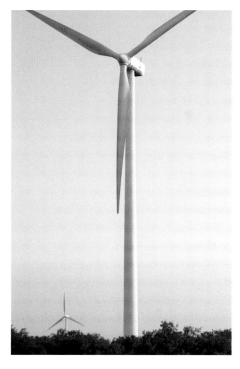

sense of new life as their blades turn gently on ridge after ridge. Coastal winds are ripe for harvest, too, so Texas has plans to develop offshore wind farms about seven miles off the coast of Galveston.

The pros of wind energy are that it is clean and renewable; the principal con is that it is not reliable and must be backed up with traditional coal and natural gas–fueled generators to supply adequate electricity.

Wind power for large-scale production of electricity has a fairly long history in Texas, beginning with wind energy research in 1970 at what is now West Texas A&M University in Canyon and with the formation of the Alternative Energy Institute in 1977. Several factors have driven the growth of wind farms: As a resource, wind is plentiful in Texas, especially in the Panhandle, along the Gulf coast south of Galveston, and in mountain passes and along

ridgetops west of the Pecos River; large projects are relatively easy to site in sparsely populated areas; and the market price is competitive with that of natural gas.

So the largest installed base of wind capacity in the nation is likely to get even bigger. That's just how things go in Texas.

American Wind Power Center and Museum | 1701 Canyon Lake Dr. | Lubbock, TX 79403
(806) 747-8734 | windmill.com

Texas Wind Power Projects | infinitepower.org/projects.htm

ACKNOWLEDGMENTS

First of all, it has been a pleasure to partner up with photographer Paul Porter on this project. He spent many man-hours crisscrossing the state capturing the visual illustrations for the icons in this book. We also acknowledge the generosity of the Texas Department of Transportation and the Texas Historical Commission, which provided photographs of Palo Duro Canyon when we were denied access because of drought-caused wildfires in the area. As always, Globe Pequot editors—in this case, Courtney Oppel, Erin Turner, and production editor Meredith Dias—provided guidelines and expertise to see the project through to completion. Much obliged, y'all.

ABOUT THE AUTHOR

A bred and born Texan, **Donna Ingham** has for many years absorbed ideas about her home state and what helps make it unique. These she continues to reflect in her oral storytelling and in her books—she has written six for Globe Pequot. A native of the Texas Panhandle and briefly a resident of the Rio Grande valley, she now lives in the Texas Hill Country in Spicewood with her husband, Jerry.

ABOUT THE PHOTOGRAPHER

When not occupied with his "real" job, **Paul Porter** can usually be found with a camera in his hands. His wife gave him a camera in 1995, and he has been taking pictures ever since. He is the official photographer of the Tejas Storytelling Association and the Lone Star Storytelling Festival, and has also done photography work for the National Storytelling Network. Paul has also cohosted a folk music concert series in the Dallas area since 1987. He lives in Duncanville with his wife, Susan Gurvich, four cats, one dog, and one parrot. More of his work can be seen at paulporter.dotphoto.com.